TABLE OF CONTENTS

DISCLAIMER AND TERMS OF USE AGREEMENT:

(Please Read This Before Using This Book)

This information is for educational and informational purposes only. The content is not intended to be a substitute for any professional advice, diagnosis, or treatment.

The authors and publisher of this book and the accompanying materials have used their best efforts in preparing this book.

The authors and publisher make no representation or warranties with respect to the accuracy, applicability, fitness, or completeness of the contents of this book. The information contained in this book is strictly for educational purposes. Therefore, if you wish to apply ideas contained in this book, you are taking full responsibility for your actions.

The authors and publisher disclaim any warranties (express or implied), merchantability, or fitness for any particular purpose. The author and publisher shall in no event be held liable to any party for any direct, indirect, punitive, special, incidental or other consequential damages arising directly or indirectly from any use of this material, which is provided "as is", and without warranties. As always, the advice of a competent legal, tax, accounting, medical or other professional should be sought where applicable.

The authors and publisher do not warrant the performance, effectiveness or applicability of any sites listed or linked to in this book. All links are for information purposes only and are not warranted for content, accuracy or any other implied or explicit purpose. No part of this may be copied, or changed in any format, or used in any way other than what is outlined within this course under any circumstances. Violators will be prosecuted.

Introduction – I Am Not the Genius Behind ForensicsNet™…sigh

I have a confession to make; I am not the genius behind ForensicsNet™. I wish I was but unfortunately I do not have expertise to design a program as comprehensive and complex as ForensicsNet™.

Yes, I am a senior cyber forensics investigator and have been one for over thirty-two years as well as a behavioral scientist and a member of ForensicsNation's AppliedMindSciences.com research unit, which is a part of ForensicsLab™ but when it comes to computer programming and writing computer code, I just don't have the skills.

Think of me as the company spokesman that will attempt to outline this formidable program and get people to be aware of it and the services that it provides. So to begin let me start by outlining exactly what the problem is and why ForensicsNet™ is needed and necessary.

Background – The Dilemma

Source Document: FNC Public Awareness Seminar PDF
http://www.filefactory.com/f/d3eac5e74de46025

Let's define terms…

Hackers – a hacker is a criminal that usually wants to make a statement but generally does no major widespread damage and is not after financial gain.

The group Anonymous is a good example. They are big at using "denial of service" attacks where they bombard a website's server until it crashes but it isn't about money.

Crackers – on the other hand, Crackers are evil and are strictly out for financial and evil gain. They are responsible for severe financial loss and stolen assets.

Stalkers – these are sexual predators bent on sexual crimes against both men, women and children. Most stalkers only follow and record their victims while remaining hidden but some will cause bodily harm.

Child Molesters – these criminals prey only on children and haunt chat rooms, video game sites, and anywhere kids hang out online.

YOU aren't the only ones being targeted! Every person, every corporate, religious and government entity is a target. Here are some examples…

Big Brother is Watching YOU

Government spying isn't accessing your computer and hacking your contents. They are directly wired into the Internet Service Providers (ISPs) and communication companies and these companies literally turn over large databases filled with your info to the NSA and other alphabet spy agencies. The trick in preventing this is called an "eraser' in forensics' lingo where all of your info, communications, pics and messages are wiped cleaned when you log off of any ISP or website.

On your personal computer or cell phone, you have the ability to erase information but it is not completely erased and in most cases it can be recovered. In forensics, the erasers we use completely wipe everything clean and nothing can be recovered. So there is a downside; we can do this for you under our FoneBlock and TechBlock programs as long as you understand that nothing can be recovered!!!

The New York Times

False Tax Returns

With Personal Data in Hand, Thieves File Early and Often

MIAMI — Besieged by identity theft, Florida now faces a fast-spreading form of fraud so simple and lucrative that some violent criminals have traded their guns for laptops. And the target is the United States Treasury.

J. Russell George, the Treasury inspector general for tax administration, testified before Congress this month that the I.R.S. **detected 940,000 fake returns for 2010 in which identity thieves would have received $6.5 billion**

in refunds. But Mr. George said the agency missed an additional 1.5 million returns with possibly fraudulent refunds worth more than $5.2 billion.

From 2008 to 2011, the number of returns filed by identity thieves and stopped by the I.R.S. increased significantly, officials said. Last year, it was at least 1.3 million, said Steven T. Miller, deputy commissioner for services and enforcement at the agency. This year, with only 30 percent of the filings reviewed so far, the number is already at 2.6 million. The bulk is related to identity theft, Mr. Miller said.

Child Abduction

FHP - *Mall* & Shopping Safety

www.flhsmv.gov/fhp/misc/christmas/mst.htm

More than 100000 *children* are *abducted* every year -- often in *malls* or department stores, according to the National Center for Missing and Exploited *Children...*

The day I was almost *abducted* & killed by a *child* predator - Kanuk ...

*open.salon.com/.../the_day_i_was_almost_**abducted**_killed_by_a_**chi**...*

Jun 22, 2010 – The day I was almost *abducted* & killed by a *child* predator **...** So I went on my way and walked to the *mall's* record store. Remember those?

Is a fifth grader old enough to go to the *mall* by himself?

And don't forget that even adult women have been *kidnapped from malls*, as well as other public places, so why would you think your *child* would be an exception...

Mail Online

And then you have what is being called "Not-So Legal Hacking of your personal info

Sinister truth about Google spies: Street View cars stole information from British households but executives 'covered it up' for years.

Work of Street View cars to be examined over allegations Google used them to download personal details.

Emails, texts, photos and documents taken from Wi-Fi networks as cars photographed British roads.

Engineer who designed software said a privacy lawyer should be consulted.

The commonality of all these cases...

The cases above are examples of cyber-crimes conducted over the Worldwide Web or Internet.

Not all cyber-crimes are for financial gain but in many cases bodily harm and even death occurs as a result.

As large as ForensicsNation is - almost 22,000 people in 22-countires - we don't even scratch the surface when it comes to cyber-crime.

Even working with counterpart companies in other countries such as Group-IB in Russia, where we share information and exchange databases, cyber-crime still runs rampant worldwide and is increasing.

http://group-ib.com/

At ForensicsNation, we go after the real bad guys...

ForensicsNation is organized into special units with expert investigators concentrating on various cyber crime activities. Here are just a few - financial, government, personal, and child molesters.

These special ops teams are highly trained and highly motivated. Using technology not available to the general public, we infiltrate and gather evidence and intelligence. This is the definition of the word "forensics" - the gathering and preservation of evidence. We then turn this evidence over to law enforcement for arrest and prosecution. But it isn't easy; cyber criminals are highly organized...

"Hunting is for fools that have never heard about bait!"

Actually the Hacker Underground is complete with their own news sites, news networks and these are really good things. These sites are where hackers BUY their information from other hackers. Info such as identity theft financial records, social security numbers, etc. So, we pose as buyers or sellers and "bait" the hackers. When they respond we plant a tracking bug into their computer systems and instantly they go into our databases.

Now you may ask how do hackers pay for this information without revealing their identities. They use the following pay sites but even their systems are not that secure (lol). They also like using offshore pay sites because they are outside the regulations of The Patriot Act.

The Problem?

So far we have briefly described some of the potential crimes you are facing. The overall problem can best be outlined using two scenarios. First is hacking or spying on your information and personal data. Second is tracking your movements using GPS technology that can result in stalking and/or bodily harm.

Both can be stopped; both can be avoided and prevented. Now we are going to show you how to take control of your privacy and protect yourself, your business and loved ones.

This isn't difficult and it is not expensive but it is necessary! Please pay close attention; privacy is a serious matter and protecting yourself from bodily harm should always be of primary concern.

The Solution?

In one word – **PREVENTION!**

And this where each and every one of you comes in!!!

By conducting our PinpointProtect® Public Awareness seminars, we educate the public and business owners of the dangers of cyber-crime and the best defense is still a good offense!

By offering our PinpointProtect® Prevention Program workshops, we can teach prevention and tactics to combat even the best cyber-criminals.

Today cyber-criminals are conducting illegal hacking, child predation, identity theft, denial of service attacks, financial fraud, online scams, phishing schemes, data theft, corporate espionage and much more...

Are you the prey or the hunter?
Give me 30-minutes and I can turn your life into a living HELL

In 30-minutes I can:

- Access your bank accounts and steal your money

- Tap your cell phone; listen to your phone calls, read your text messages.

- I can track your movements using GPS

- I can learn all about you – where you live, where you work, your habits, if you are single or married, your kid's names and ages, EVERYTHING!

- I can access your social media and change your profile and pics

- I can post false information about you that will never come off the net.

- I can find out your religious affiliation, voting records, and more.

- I will know your car, license info, and insurance data.

In short, give me 30-minutes and I will know everything about you and you cannot stop me because all of this info is on the Internet and you will never know who I am because I can hide where nobody will find me.

Now you know why our compliance people watch us very carefully.

Although truth lives a wretched life, it outlives a lie every time!

Sooner or later truth always prevails and our job at ForensicsNation is to find the truth.

We have a saying, "An investigation doesn't end until someone is in handcuffs!" and we are well known for our tenacity.

But as we said before, as good as we are we need your help to combat the ever-increasing rate of cyber-crime. **Forewarned is forearmed!**

So now, allow us to describe cyber crime in terms of how it can affect you and introduce you to our programs that protect you.

All of what I am about to describe is in the aforementioned download portal that we will give you at the end of this presentation.

Enter ForensicsNation...

Because of the nature of what we do, our forensic investigators are cloaked in anonymity for their personal protection as well as their families.

The PinpointProtect® Prevention Program is important and so are the prevention products that we introduce to combat cyber-crime.

We have spent the better part of 32-years in Cyber-Forensics and we have a good deal experience with cyber criminal activity.

What makes cyber-crime so ominous is the fact that cyber-criminals choose to hide behind their computer terminals and never actually witness the damage and harm that they do.

They are not just immoral but cowards with absolutely no empathy for anybody including themselves.

#1 Target of Hackers and Crackers: LAW ENFORCEMENT

ForensicsNation's website is subject to hacker attacks hourly...

And I mean HOURLY!!! And candidly we LOVE IT too!

Why?

Because every hacker attack is monitored and defended by our compliance people and our internal security people and we plant spy software on the hacker's computer to reverse engineer their attack.

Now we have another hacker in our databanks to go after.

But most law enforcement agencies do not have our technology and protection so they are penetrated daily.

Law enforcement officers worldwide have their cell phones compromised. At ForensicsNation, our investigator's cell phones are scanned hourly for spyware.

It truly is a jungle out there.

Everything cops have and use is unprotected

Anonymous's release of Met and FBI call puts hacker group back centre stage

Activist collective's leak of 18-minute discussion embarrasses authorities and raises questions over how security was breached

Josh Halliday and Charles Arthur
guardian.co.uk, Friday 3 February 2012 11.37 EST

Anonymous' release of a phone call between the Met police and the FBI has embarrassed the authorities. Photograph: Suzanne Webber/Rex Features

The hacking collective Anonymous has struck deep into the heart of one of its sworn enemies – the police – with the release of the recording of a conference call between the Metropolitan police and the FBI. In it, they discuss ongoing investigations and court cases against alleged British hackers; and now, courtesy of Anonymous, the world can listen in too.

#2 Target of Hackers and Crackers: YOU!

Hackers and Crackers go after YOU in this order of importance

1. **Children** – predators are most active in child abduction and abuse.

2. **Women** – everything from stalking to voyeurism to sex slavery.

3. **Businesses** – small business are more often targeted due to less protective measures.

4. **General Population** – in the form of various cyber crimes such as identity theft, computer intrusion, and phishing scams.

5. **Government Agencies** – patient records on file with state record keepers getting hacked.

Areas of Personal EXPOSURE
- Credit Card Fraud

- Identity Theft

- Financial Scams

- Child Predation

- Computer Hijacking

- Malware, Spyware

- Electronic Voyeurism

- Viruses

- Keystroke Logging

- Phishing

- User Account & Password Theft

- Cell Phone Spying

- Online Auction Fraud – Ebay, etc.

- And much more…

The above areas of personal exposure are the more prevalent forms of cyber crimes directed against individuals. It is by no means a complete list.

YOU are the target!

Surfing the Web - One way that hackers get hold of you is when you surf the web. They put up enticing websites and as soon as you bring one up on your screen they are secretly downloading spyware onto your computer.

Cell Phone Spying - One of the easiest ways to become a victim of cyber-crime is by hacking into your cell phone and installing spyware. Today's Cell Phone spyware does not require that the hacker have possession of your phone. They simply text or call your cell phone number and whether it is answered or not, it takes all of about 30-seconds to marry your phone to the spyware. Spyware of this type is readily available on the open market.

Did you know that with the help of a simple, inexpensive device, anyone with access to your phone could read your private text messages (SMS), even if you have deleted them previously? This device can even recover contacts and previously dialed numbers. There is also a device that costs a whopping $20 that will tell you the cell phone number of any cell phone within 40-feet of the device. And "no" we are NOT going to tell you where to buy one!!!

Cyber Criminals are waiting for you!

Email - Your email accounts can quite easily be hacked. There is software available on the open market that breaks usernames and passwords. Also, if your computer is hacked, most people leave sensitive information on their computer that can fall into a hacker's hands.

Hard Drive Intrusion - Hacking your hard drive and other data storage devices can be prevented by using disc encryption programs.

Other Areas of Vulnerability- Firewalls, Internet Phone, Chat rooms, PORN, computer hijacking and much more…

DO NOT USE ANY OF THE FREE EMAIL SERVICES SUCH AS GMAIL, YAHOO OR HOTMAIL!!! What you want is a private email service like the one above that you can access from the Internet under an "https" link. ForensicsNation offers a secure and protected email address with unlimited web access for just $4.97/month. Example: suzie@forensicsnation.com. To order, download the FNC Catalog here: http://www.filefactory.com/f/d3eac5e74de46025

The Ever-Increasing Cyber Problem

The main problem is that the average computer user has no idea that they are exposed and even if they do, they have no idea how to protect themselves.

As technology expands, the tools available to the hacker and cyber-criminal expand too. They keep up with everything on the Internet where the average user does not.

Cyber-criminals are organizing into gangs. The most famous is the hacking gang called Anonymous that used

"Denial of Service" techniques against major financial institutions that denied Wikileaks merchant account facilities in 2011.

But in countries such as Russia and many of the old "iron curtain" countries too, organized cyber-crime gangs are increasing.

The 10-Most Notorious Cyber Gangs

1-Russian Business Network

2-Rock Phish Gang

3-NSA

4-Grey Pigeon Authors

5-Stormworm Gang

6-Awola Crew

7-DRG Group

8-South American Groups

9-Oga-Nigerian

10-Individual Hackers (Anonymous)

As cyber-crime increases, so does their income and this feeds the increase of more cyber-crime. Like drugs, cyber-crime pays and it pays very well.

*****

ForensicsNation.com is a 32-year old private forensics investigative company with over 22,000 forensics investigators in over 22-countires worldwide specializing in cyber crimes of all types. Its international headquarters is based in Lugano, Switzerland with North American Operations based in Deland, Florida.

The increase in cyber-crime worldwide has caused a major problem in the law enforcement ranks. All law enforcement entities combined cannot make an effective dent in cyber-crime to date. The answer to this dilemma is prevention. ForensicsNation.com has created a cloud-based security net that protects it member participants from all forms of cyber-crime and cyber penetration and it works in conjunction with a state of the art forensics lab integrated into its daily operation.

Forensicsnation.com offers a free online Public Awareness seminar that demonstrates the worldwide cyber-crime threat. Go to http://www.addmeinnow.com to sign up for the free 56-minute online seminar.

ForensicsNation.com also offers an online catalog of products (most of which are FREE) that allows users to protect themselves from most but not all cyber-crimes. Go here to download the FNC Catalog:

http://www.filefactory.com/f/110d62a5a3dcf84b

Chapter 1 – You Are Not Alone!

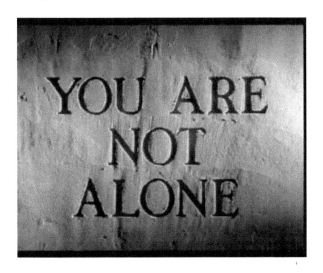

What could you possibly have in common with the celebrities pictured below? Celebrities such as Oprah Winfrey, Paris Hilton, Michael Jordan, Tiger Woods, Franklin Delano Roosevelt, Steven Spielberg, Barry Bonds, Ted Turner, Warren Buffet, Mayor Michael Bloomberg, Robert De Niro, Martha Stewart, Will Smith, Ross Perot, Football star Ty Law, Disney CEO Michael Eisner, Pro-basketball player Steve Smith, Law & Order star Jerry Orbach, Quarterback Danny Wuerfful, Novelist Grahame Greene, Oracle boss Larry Ellison, Motown star Martha Reeves, American Idol Ruben Studdard.

Well if you are a victim of cyber-crime and every year there are 10-million new victims of cyber-crime in the

United States alone then you have one thing in common with all the celebrities cited below.

They have all been victims of cyber-crimes...mostly identity theft!

Tiger Woods

Ty Law

Ricky Gervais

Ruben Studdard

Michael Bloomberg

27

Lily Allen

Will Smith

Steve Smith

Liv Tyler

Oprah Winfrey

Identity theft is a fairly common problem for celebrities, actors, musicians, CEO's, athletes and politicians. Living in the public eye makes you an easy target for identity thieves.

Here is a good online resource to read…Identity Theft: http://blog.credit.com/identity-theft/

*****

ID thief to the stars tells all
http://www.nbcnews.com/id/5763781

Book excerpt: In "Your Evil Twin," MSNBC.com's Bob Sullivan argues that credit industry neglect led to the identity theft epidemic

Note: Last year, some 10 million people were victims of identity theft, and some estimates claim as many as 1 in 10 Americans have been hit by the crime in recent years. MSNBC.com's Bob Sullivan explores the digital epidemic in a new book, "Your Evil Twin." Chapter 1 begins with confessions from perhaps the world's most infamous ID thief, James Rinaldo Jackson, who seemingly impersonated half of Wall Street and half of Hollywood during his 20-year career.

"It's so very simple to be anyone you please, on any given morning you awake." —James Rinaldo Jackson

As the CEO of a Hollywood studio, Terry Semel certainly didn't want to be bothered at home by budding writers peddling two-bit scripts. His home phone number was unlisted. His assistants at Warner Bros. knew better than to give out his address. In 1993, well before the popularization of the Internet, before fan stalker web sites existed, before nationwide telephone lookups were just a few mouse clicks away, maintaining an unlisted number offered reasonable protection against crackpots and fanatics.

So Semel, today the CEO of Yahoo! Inc., must have been surprised that day in 1993 when a Federal Express package arrived at his home. Inside was, of course, a movie pitch from a would-be screen writer. Film producers are used to seeing all manner of desperate attempts to get their attention, but this pitch was very different. As Semel shuffled through the papers, perhaps he realized that he was staring at a shocking mirror of himself, or rather, of his financial self. Somehow, the screenwriter had sent Semel a copy of his Social Security number, bank account number, credit card number, and part of his credit report. And that was just the beginning. Semel turned the pages and found dozens of other digital dossiers, all manner of personal data not meant for his eyes belonging to a Who's Who in Hollywood: Steven Segal, Mel Gibson, Michael Ovitz, Danny DeVito, Sydney Pollack, Leonard Nimoy, and the screenwriter's favorite, Steven Spielberg. Next to each name were private financial account numbers, mother's maiden names, itemized purchases from credit card billing statements, and more.

"There are leaks in the system," the letter said. The author was an inmate at the Millington, Tennessee, federal prison camp. The prisoner wanted a movie deal. But with the offer came what sounded like a warning: Someone is planning to commit a massive fraud against all these famous people, it said. Lawrence Tisch, Arsenio Hall, Tom Cruise, Lew Wasserman, Alan Ladd, and many others. They were all on a hit list. Someone should do something. Perhaps a movie would help. The prisoner understood better than most what was about to happen to our digital world. His tone in this letter was at once childlike and prophetic. In one breath, he pitches his wife "Princess" and his friends for roles in the movie. In the next, he describes the coming billion-dollar crisis. Perhaps that's why no one took the June 1, 1993, correspondence very seriously.

"Millions of citizens across America have been or will become victims of fraudulent activities caused by other criminal-minded individuals," he wrote. "In other aspects, illegal purchases of real estate, expensive automobiles, and fine jewelry and easy access to other people's bank accounts, credit cards. . . . It's time for these matters to be dealt with on a more realistic basis and put to a screeching halt."

A Spielberg fan

James Rinaldo Jackson is, among other things, a Steven Spielberg fanatic. Such a fanatic, in fact, that for an entire year in the mid-1990s, he knew everything Spielberg purchased on his American Express card. "He has awesome taste, class, and style you won't believe," Jackson says now about Spielberg.

Everything Jackson learned about Spielberg, he learned while in prison, much of it using a cell phone supplied by a family member. Jackson says he never tried to steal anything from the famous Hollywood director. He just wanted to snoop. "When you like and admire someone of his phenomenal talent, you don't even attempt to step on his shoes," he said. But you might drop his name, and some personal data, to get the attention of a big movie producer. Just a few calls while in the care of the federal prison system, and Jackson scored all sorts of data on Spielberg and about 100 other Hollywood types. All in a single day's work.

He started by calling the Screen Actors Guild and tricking an operator into sharing the name of the guild's health care insurance provider. Then he called the provider's toll-free number and pretended to be an administrator at a medical provider looking to verify

33

coverage for billing purposes. Helpful operators spat back Social Security numbers, dates of birth, addresses, and other private information. "All I needed was a name," he said. Then, he would start his "prowl."

"I called up American Express. The rep asked me for my account number when I gave him my name as Steven Spielberg. He was a young-sounding guy who appeared to be overwhelmed and excited to a degree until he asked me, 'Is this the Steven Spielberg?' "Calmly, my reply was no. Then I said, 'I'm mistaken for him every single day of my life.' "So he relaxed somewhat and proceeded to ask me for my account number when I told him I didn't have my card with me at the time. Then I remember saying something to the effect of, 'Unfortunately I left home without mine, I'm certain the real Steven Spielberg would never do such.' "After I told him that, he said, 'Well, that's okay, how about your Social Security number?' Thanks to the Screen Actors Guild, I had that. So I called out all nine digits. Then the rep asked me for my date of birth and I gave him that. The rep then went on to say 'How can I help you?' I asked for my balance, which was nearly $100,000. Then the representative started to give me a detailed billing of the charges, where he had dined, establishments where the card had been used, amount of last payment, current payment due. This guy had real good taste. He spent wads of money on brand-name clothes and expensive jewelry, wined and dined at the top-of-the-line hotels. . . ."

Fraud from a jail cell

It took a year before guards discovered Jackson was committing identity fraud while behind bars. On daily outdoor work duty at a nearby military base, Jackson had only his memory of toll-free phone numbers and payphones to work with. Still, he managed to score stolen credit card accounts and other funds from a host of wealthy people. Other inmates helped; accomplices who stood guard while he made the phone calls were paid off with pizza, beer, Nike sneakers, jogging suits, jewelry, watches, even money, all funded by credit card accounts pilfered over the telephone. They even watched his back so he could find time alone with a blue eyed, blonde-haired female Naval officer stationed on the base. When their love affair was ratted out, he was sent to solitary confinement.

Later, he was only allowed work detail near the prison, doing simple landscaping and garbage collecting under the constant watchful eye of prison guards. But even that didn't stop him. Jackson's brother-in-law drove up one day, discarded a crumpled- up fast-food bag, and missed the trash. Jackson picked it up, as was the plan, and later took out the cell phone and car charger that had been left inside. He could chat on the phone while sitting in the prison's landscaping truck, which he was still allowed to drive around the compound. He hid the phone inside the truck's air vents when he left. The scheme worked for a few months, until Jackson got too greedy yet again— when he tried to steal thousands of dollars from Dean Witter executives, including CEO Charles Fiumeffredo, he set off red flags. It meant another two years in a federal prison, and finally, he said, "I was put inside a place with barbed wire." Only then did he temporarily stop posing as America's elite for his own financial gain; but it was just a temporary hiatus.

A few months after his release in 1998, he would be back at it again. His best work was still ahead of him. While he did get the thrill of being Steven Spielberg for a while, Jackson never got his movie deal. He did have several telephone conversations with an assistant to Terry Semel at Warner Brothers during several weeks in 1993, who encouraged Jackson. But shortly after that, Jackson was moved to another prison where he had no phone privileges, and he lost contact with the movie studio. "I didn't get the movie deal because identity theft wasn't a major concern . . . back then," Jackson said. "I felt then it would eventually become a fast-growing crime in America. And it did!" As if to fulfill his own prophesy, Jackson ended up scamming some of the famous people on the list he sent to Semel. Many never knew Jackson was the culprit, even though he should have been an obvious suspect, given the typewritten preconfession. Victims from the Semel letter include Robert and Patricia Stemple, then CEO of General Motors; and CBS's Lawrence Tisch. "I'm extremely remorseful," he says now, addressing the victims. "Please forgive me."

Obsessed with Elvis

James Rinaldo Jackson had an unusual childhood for Memphis, Tennessee in the 1960s. His mother was black and his father white; at school, he was quickly given the nickname, "Zebra," and it stuck. The teasing was painful, but young James turned the tables by embracing the label. At times, he remembers refusing to answer when his

36

parents called him James–he insisted that his name was "Zebra." Then, when he was given a guitar for Christmas, he began imagining he was a member of the Beatles. Call me John, Paul, or Ringo, he demanded. Like many kids, he would break out in song, blaring, "She loves you, yeah, yeah, yeah!" and not always at the most appropriate of times. His parents laughed it off; his babysitter spanked him when she got irritated, but no one really took notice how much energy James put into being other people. Or how good he was getting at it.

His musical affections quickly turned local, and Elvis became the target of his obsession. By the time he was 12, he insisted on eating jelly donuts, peanut butter sandwiches topped with banana slices, and wearing blue suede shoes for special occasions. One day, his father told him, gently, that "God made you and there's only one you in the whole wide world," attempting to urge the boy to start to find his own personality. But it was devastating for James, who realized then that there must be only one Elvis, too. He says he burst into tears at the kindly remark. "That man doesn't know what he's talking about," James remembers thinking. "He's got life all wrong."

By a stroke of luck, Jackson attended Humes Jr. High, where Elvis had attended high school. The obsession became complete. He even imagined he was crapping in the same place Elvis did. "I wanted to say that I sat bare butt on the same toilet (Elvis had), to describe the wonderful feeling of sensation from the rim of a commode where Elvis sat," Jackson wrote in a private memoir he hopes to publish some day. He would end up in detention for creating disruptions as he broke out into Elvis songs during school.

Just as James was about to reach high school, his father died suddenly. Now he felt he had something else in common with The King, who had lost his mother when he was still young. James remembers staring at Elvis' retired football jersey in the school's trophy case, crying, and singing "That's All right Mama" to himself. He prayed for his dad and his mom, and soon vowed to transfer schools so he could get away from his overwhelming desire to be someone else. But his attempt at self-rehabilitation didn't last, because right about then he learned that he could make good money pretending to be other people. And with his father now gone, his mother sure could use the help.

It began innocently enough. The golden age of rock-and-roll radio brought with it intense competition and stations quickly learned the best way to steal listeners from each other was to pay them. Cash giveaways and other prize games were everywhere. Just by knowing what songs the stations were playing, and calling at the right time, James could win $300 at a clip.

Sometimes he won five prizes a day, calling shows in the morning before school. His most prized winnings at the time was a ladies' Wittnauer watch worth $150, which he was able to give his mom as a present when he was only 15 years old. Of course, 15-year-olds weren't supposed to win; and no one was eligible to win contests repeatedly each day. James says he beat the system by setting up a bank of telephones at home and quick-dialing them repeatedly, by hand, so he could be caller number 10. Then, when he won, he would disguise his voice–sometimes as a 90-year-old grandmother, sometimes a young, excitable woman. And he would use various names and addresses all over town. Next, he'd simply wait for the valuable mail to arrive, sneak into the mailbox, and collect his winnings. He also won free blenders, toasters, grills, kitchen ware and other appliances for his family. At the time, he felt "the ability to talk my way out of anything I wanted or for that matter, talk my way into retrieving anything I wanted, too."

Jackson didn't last long in college; instead, his true college was the University Club of Memphis, where he waited tables on the rich and famous from his teen years to his early 20s. Charming, exceedingly polite, and patient, he learned how to talk the way powerful people talk, with confidence and back-slapping humor always at ready disposal. He also learned to dislike the smug elite, and he acquired a taste for outsmarting people who were supposed to be smarter than him.

From the Federal Correctional Institution in Forrest City, Arkansas, where he is serving an 8-year term for his most recent frauds, Jackson, for the first time, offered elaborate details of his 15-year identity fraud crime spree. Fueled by a burning desire to demonstrate that he is sorry for his crimes, which could reduce his prison term, Jackson agreed to a lengthy set of correspondence interviews, offering an intimate look at criminal imposters and the broken systems that enable them.

"It's 7:06 A.M., I've had my M&Ms, it's time to exert some positive energy," he wrote. The perfectly typed, single-spaced letters of about four thousand words each could have as few as two paragraphs and contained even fewer typing mistakes. "As the ole saying goes, the early bird gets the worm. . . ."

An Oprah fan

To say that Jackson is star struck would be quite an understatement. In the early 1990s, just as Oprah Winfrey's stock was headed from star to superstar, Jackson learned that Oprah's father owned a barbershop in Nashville, a couple of hundred miles away from Memphis. No matter; Jackson decided he just had to have his hair cut by Vernon Winfrey. More than a decade later, he still remembers their first encounter in vivid detail. One of the other barbers had an open chair and offered it to him; he refused, of course. When Winfrey's chair came open, he turned on the charm. "I've never had my hair cut by the father of a famous daughter," Jackson said, getting just a little laugh.

Then, the two bantered back and forth about Jackson's hometown of Memphis and Winfrey's whimsical idea that the city should really be part of Mississippi. After all, Oprah was born in Mississippi. Jackson remembers driving to the barbershop in his stolen pearl-white Mercedes Benz 420 SEL. Winfrey, who noticed the car, said his daughter had recently bought him a similar Mercedes, a 560 SEL with heated seats and a bigger engine. He didn't like driving it, though, because it didn't fit in well with the neighborhood, a poor section of Music

City. Eventually, Jackson learned Winfrey still lived in the tough area, which Jackson called "the hood," despite Oprah's recent gift of an expansive, half-million-dollar mansion in the suburbs. "He told me that Oprah nearly begged him and begged him to move into the home; he kept putting it off . . . he point blank said to me, 'James, that's my daughter's money and fame. I am so happy right here where I am, where I've been living among average, everyday kind of people nearly all my life. I don't need all of that.'" He went on to say that Oprah had offered to buy him a brand new barbershop, or to rebuild the one he had, but he refused.

On the Winfrey barbershop is a wall with thousands of pictures from well-wishers who have stopped by to meet the famous father. Before he left, Jackson thanked Winfrey for being gracious, shook his hand, gave Winfrey his picture, and then waited to make sure it ended up on that wall. The elder Winfrey's kindly ways probably saved his daughter a financial headache in the future. Jackson, a sort of digital-age Robin Hood, declared Oprah off-limits after the visit. "He was an amazingly warm and sensible gentleman that I grew to love, admire, and respect all because he treated me like a customer who was there spending a million bucks on fine, fine jewels," Jackson says now. "It made me not ever want to commit an identity theft crime against anyone that had close ties to Mr. Winfrey." Others among the world's famous and elite weren't so lucky.

He started small, rigging car accident claims involving rented cars in the late 1980s. With a band of disciples in tow, he honed that craft and ultimately staged some 50 accidents, netting the crime gang $642,000. But car accidents were hard work, and another, more lucrative money-making scheme was emerging. While working as a delivery driver for Federal Express, Jackson met a Nigerian "professor" who explained the ins and outs of the insurance industry and the methods for tricking customer service telephone operators into divulging critical data on anyone. Watching CNN one night in the late 1980s, he saw Time Warner's Gerald Levine being interviewed and decided to give it a whirl. Moments later, he had a full digital dossier on Levine. It was as easy as lying to the man's health insurance company. Within two years, Jackson had worked his way through much of corporate America, impersonating such luminaries as Edward Brennan, CEO of Sears, Charles Lebreque, former head of Chase, and about 25 other CEOs, which he still won't discuss.

But he had his biggest early score by hitting a victim in his own backyard. The Belz family is one of the most influential real estate developers in the south—certainly in Memphis, Tennessee, where the family owns a series of malls and office complexes. But no one noticed in 1990 when Jackson stole a letter addressed to Jack Belz, then CEO of Belz Associates, and applied for a credit card in Belz's name. He managed some $116,000 in purchases and cash withdrawals on credit cards in Belz's name before he was finally stopped.

In the meantime, he was living in style, chilling in a $150,000 home he had purchased in Georgia using a false ID. He had amassed an impressive fleet of luxury cars via identity theft. In addition to the Mercedes, he had a

Lincoln Continental, a BMW, and a Nissan Pathfinder. A Corvette he once owned had been exchanged for a Lotus Esprit SE. The women came easily, too, especially when he wasn't paying. Jackson says he regularly carried FBI and U.S. Marshal Service credentials that often earned him free sex. When he checked into hotels, he got into the habit of flipping through the yellow pages and calling a local escort service, ordering one or two girls at a time. When he was finished with them, he'd let them dress and then flash a badge "smack dab in the middle of their face," read them their rights, and announce a sting. He'd offer to let the girls go if they returned his money. He'd even make a crank call and carry the gag further, until they returned the cash. "It worked like a charm 99.5 percent of the times I pulled this scheme," he wrote. "The other 0.5 percent nearly cost me my life."

Beginning of the end

While pimps never caught up with Jackson, the cops eventually did. Law enforcement agencies began to circle Jackson in late 1990, and his world would begin to unravel the next year. Insurance investigators from Geico and a local furniture store he had bilked had him arrested. But perhaps as a bit of poetic license, his first conviction involved theft of airline travel, using a technique not unlike that of famed impersonator Frank Abignale. Jackson had assumed the identity of a Federal Express employee with the same name and had been flying around the country for under $50, round trip, using the other Jackson's employee discounts. When he was arrested, federal authorities also found a $55,000 Cadillac Allante and a $40,000 Lexus in his driveway, both purchased using fake Social Security numbers. Court documents indicate he was arrested with a series of credit cards under assumed names, including "those of top executives of major U.S. corporations."

While awaiting trial, Jackson continued to show his ability to acquire hard-to-find information. The master imposter sought revenge against the FBI agent who helped catch him, reporting a domestic disturbance at the agent's home. Jackson called from jail, telling dispatchers someone had been stabbed inside the agent's home during a family fight. The address was supposed to be a federal secret. But soon a sheriff, an ambulance, and several fire trucks were outside the agent's home. He messed with my family, I'll mess with his, Jackson said at the time, according to court documents.

Later, to convince Judge Julia Smith Gibbons that conditions inside the jail where he was being held were unlivable, Jackson sent a box full of bugs, which were gathered in his cell, to the judge's home. Thanks in part to such jail-cell shenanigans, he found himself in federal custody for the next seven years.

Chapter 2 – Hunting Is For Fools Who Have Never Heard About Bait!

To be very clear, forensics is defined as the compilation and preservation of evidence and in cyber-forensics, we add an additional definition of identification and apprehension of the perpetrator(s).

Our methods, modalities and tactics are classified and cannot not be divulged but I want to make one thing perfectly clear – cyber-forensic agents NEVER hunt perpetrators or suspects – WE BAIT THEM and hence the title of this chapter.

Hunting people takes a good amount of time and personnel. It is a good deal easier to bait criminals using a good many techniques that ForensicsNation's people have designed and created and it works very well.

Here is an example: many of you have become aware of the various credit card breaches at Target, Nordstrom's, Michaels and more. Literally millions of credit card accounts and data were stolen as a result of a program written by a teenage cyber hacker located in Eastern Europe.

Within days the stolen information was put up for sale on a variety of hacker sites worldwide. Here is an opportunity of a good cyber forensics agent to pose as a buyer and penetrate the hacker's network.

Like the FBI and many of the law enforcement agencies worldwide, we identify the hacker and cracker but rarely move in and arrest them immediately. What usually occurs is that we wait and watch how they do business, who they work with, what targets they are attempting to penetrate, and the methods of operation.

It is important to learn their levels of skills and sophistication. Furthermore, it is important to determine if they are part of a vast network or cyber gang as described in the Introduction and who, what and where they go for assistance.

Cyber gangs and hackers and crackers of all types interface with others in vast underground networks as you will learn when you watch the FREE Online Public Awareness seminar also in the Introduction of this book.

The tactics and strategies used by ForensicsNation's personal causes a very high arrest and apprehension rate of cyber criminals of all types. ForensicsNation works very closely with many law enforcement agencies worldwide and share our vast databases with them also.

As the photo above demonstrates, baiting perpetrators is used by law enforcement in many different types of scenarios and is not just reserved for cyber crime.

Now, in the next chapter I will describe in detail exactly what ForensicsNet™ and ForensicsLab™ is and how users benefit from placing all of their "stuff" in this formidable cloud based security net.

Chapter 3 – What Exactly Is ForensicsNet™ and ForensicsLab™?

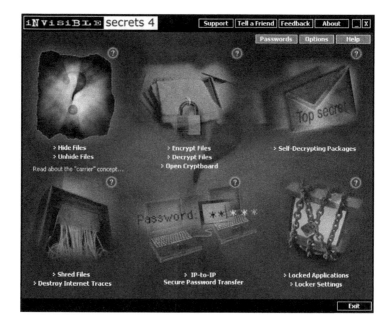

ForensicsNet™ - A Cloud-based Security Net

The cloud-based security net (hereinafter called ForensicsNet™ ™) allows participants to add in all computer-related applications, mobile applications, hardware applications and research applications in an easy user interface.

ForensicsNet™ is fully encrypted in a never before see encryption application that changes every 30-seconds and offers complete safety and protection to its users.

It is virtually impossible to invade ForensicsNet™ because it is scanned 24/7 everyday for penetration and intrusion attempts and is constantly monitored by ForensicsNation personnel.

Being cloud-based, ForensicsNet™ can be accessed by its members/users worldwide in an easy and efficient manner using a simple user interface. Adding any type of application, folder or database to ForensicsNet™ is simple and quick.

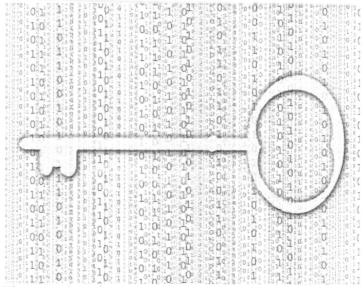

The user interface employs a "drag and drop" feature where the user can easily place any file, folder, application, into the cloud, etc by simply clicking on what needs to be placed in the cloud and dragging it into the cloud box on the website. You can also remove anything placed in the cloud using the same user interface.

ForensicsLab™

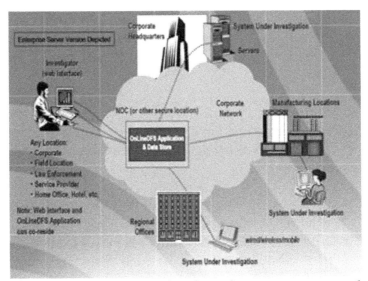

ForensicsLab™ is an online forensics scanner constantly scanning anything place in the ForensicsNet™ cloud to determine if is disguised as an intruder/cyber crime penetration.

ForensicsNation employs various scanning and surveillance programs and scans the entire internet especially targeting dating sites, sites frequented by child, free email sites, etc and uses a wide variety of scanning techniques to uncover cyber penetrations, intrusions, stalkers, sexual predators and much more. The scanning programs used for these types of operations are not the same as ForensicsLab™.

ForensicsLab™ is the new generation of scanning software designed especially for ForensicsNet™. Candidly, it is an understatement to describe ForensicsLab™ as a new generation of scanning software. There is nothing in the world today that even

51

comes close to ForensicsLab™'s capabilities and versatility. I cannot describe the capabilities of ForensicsLab™ in further detail because of the "top secret" design of this software.

Suffice it to say that ForensicsLab™ is virtually unstoppable and there is no software available anywhere in the world today that can prevent ForensicsLab™ from doing its job.

ForensicsLab™ is a computer software program. Below is an onsite forensics lab, which is used for all types of crimes except cyber crime. ForensicsNation has one main onsite forensics lab based in St. George, Utah.

In addition, ForensicsNation employs over three dozen mobile forensics labs that can travel to any crime site and do on location forensics analysis.

Now I want to introduce you to the two people responsible for the concept and creation of ForensicsNet™ /ForensicsLab™ - Drs. Leland Benton and Harry Jay.

Chapter 4 – Meet the ForensicsNation Super Hackers of All Time

I can surely bet that the two individuals I am about to describe to you are not going to like being labeled "super hackers" but the individual sums of their talent let alone the combined talents of these two individuals places them in a class by themselves and there is no better word in the English language to describe them but "super hackers" so I will apologize in advance to both of them and will demonstrate exactly what I mean.

As stated previously, ForensicsNation has over 22,000 forensic investigators worldwide and heading up this vast force is Chief Forensic Investigator Dr. Leland Benton. The training that Leland and his team provide is second to none and in actuality all 22,000 plus ForensicsNation investigators can all be called super hackers too since they are trained to identify cyber criminals of all types and use hacking skills to collect and preserve evidence.

But with that said, ForensicsNation has two divisions that watch all personnel 24/7 and these two divisions are the compliance unit and the legal division. All ForensicsNation personnel are monitored 24/7 not only to ensure they are not doing something they shouldn't be doing but also for security purposes too.

Now back to Leland…

Leland has been a forensic investigator for over thirty two years and a computer system programmer for almost the same amount of time.

Leland relies heavily on Dr. Harry Jay, whose computer talents are even greater than Leland's talents. Leland's main talents revolve around management and creative design and implementation.

Dr. Harry Jay is the programming genius behind ForensicsNet™ /ForensicsLab™ and Harry was responsible for almost 90% of the vast amount of written computer code for both programs. Both programs are modular in their design architecture and this enables easier monitoring of all internal systems.

Dr. Harry Jay is also a Chief Forensic Investigator like Leland but specializes in online sexual predators. In his book, "Confessions of a Child Predator" he describes one of his toughest child predator investigation and after the arrest and conviction; he interviewed the two woman that were responsible for multiple teenage deaths. This is a very interesting book: http://www.amazon.com/dp/B007BB97KU and I recommend this book as one that is simply fantastic.

Harry's book is just one part of ePubWealth's forensics series. Here is the complete series:

Cyber Crime/Cyber Forensics
Confessions of a Child Predator
http://www.amazon.com/dp/B007BB97KU
Child Watch
http://www.amazon.com/dp/B0095K1P3M
Cyber-Daters Beware
http://www.amazon.com/dp/B006J9T4NA
Cyber Protect Your Business
http://www.amazon.com/dp/B0095JEAYY
ForensicsNation Bushwhacker Program
http://www.amazon.com/dp/B007I9AHVS

ForensicsNation Catalog
http://www.filefactory.com/f/d3eac5e74de46025
Hackers and Crackers
http://www.amazon.com/dp/B00EXQ0HDC
Judgment Not Included
http://www.amazon.com/dp/B00CPRSQ3E
Protecting Yourself from Cyber Crime
http://www.amazon.com/dp/B0095J3EIW
Sleeping with Guns
http://www.amazon.com/dp/B00CS1IBZU
Stealing You
http://www.amazon.com/dp/B00778TT6E
The Mind Of a Con Man
http://www.amazon.com/dp/B00CO2BQHI
Was Sandy Hook a Hoax?
http://www.amazon.com/dp/B00BFSM8IS
Why Women Should Not Use Online Dating Services
http://www.amazon.com/dp/B006J9EMH8
You Can Run But You Cannot Hide
http://www.amazon.com/dp/B006JLVZC6

In the development and design of ForensicsNet™ /ForensicsLab™, Leland was responsible for the basic design configuration concept while Harry took what Leland needed and made it a reality.

Looking at the original design, a good many changes have been made based on new problems that have occurred within the cyber crime field and new targets that have surfaced.

One of the most intriguing aspects to ForensicsNet™ /ForensicsLab™ is that its modular design allows for quick adjustment to new threats worldwide.

Now let's move on to what exactly ForensicsNet™ /ForensicsLab™ does protect...

Chapter 5 – Like It or Not; You Are A Target!

Every year over ten million Americans become victims of cyber crime and the number is increasing exponentially every year. Since the economic downturn in 2008, cyber crime has been increasing because barriers to entry are almost nil and it is extremely profitable. I personally have noticed that some people are engaging in cyber crimes that were law-abiding citizens prior to the economic downturn. In other words, some people are turning to cyber crime to make ends meet and get caught in the clutches of greed.

Hackers and crackers have an entire subculture to rely on for resources and training. They even have their own newsletter. Here is one of my books that explains it all called Hackers and Crackers http://www.amazon.com/dp/B00EXQ0HDC.

Candidly, people become victims because they make it so easy for hackers and crackers to attack them. Most people do not have any protection whatsoever nor are they even aware of the threats facing them.

Go to http://www.addmeinnow.com and sign up for ForensicsNation's FREE Online Public Awareness Seminar. It is about 56-minutes long and you will thank me afterwards. It is free so you have no excuse to not watch it.

Also download the FREE FNC Catalog with oodles of free programs that you can use to protect yourself including your children. Go here to download the FNC Catalog:

FNC Catalog
http://www.filefactory.com/f/110d62a5a3dcf84b

Furthermore, ForensicsNet™ /ForensicsLab™ is not yet open and available to the public. To be notified by email when the program launchers sign up here:

http://forms.aweber.com/form/88/1351406188.htm

*****

I want to make you aware of a great article from http://www.staysafeonline.org and it is available in PDF format:

http://www.staysafeonline.org/stay-safe-online/resources/victims-of-cybercrime-tip-sheet

Victims of Cybercrime (PDF)

To view or download a PDF version, click here: http://www.staysafeonline.org/download/datasets/4292/victim_of_cybercrime_tip_sheet.pdf

The Realities of Cybercrime

When dealing with cybercrime, an ounce of prevention is truly worth a pound of cure. Cybercrime in all its many forms (e.g., online identity theft, financial fraud, stalking, bullying, hacking, e-mail spoofing, information piracy and forgery, intellectual property crime, and more) can, at best, wreak havoc in victims' lives through major inconvenience and annoyance. At worst, cybercrime can lead to financial ruin and potentially threaten a victim's reputation and personal safety.

It's always wise to do as much as possible to prevent cybercrime.

One of the best ways to learn how to prevent cybercrime is to check out **STOP. THINK. CONNECT.** at http://stopthinkconnect.org/tips-and-advice/.

But, despite our best efforts, our increasingly digital lives may put us in harm's way. The fact remains that the bad guys continue to find new uses for ever-expanding—but easily accessible—online technologies to steal, harass, and commit all sorts of crime. If cybercrime happens to you, you need to know what to do and to respond quickly.

Should I Report Cybercrime?

Cybercrime can be particularly difficult to investigate and prosecute because it often crosses legal jurisdictions and even international boundaries. And, many offenders disband one online criminal operation—only to start up a new activity with a new approach—before an incident even comes to the attention of the authorities.

The good news is that federal, state, and local law enforcement authorities are becoming more sophisticated about and devoting more resources to responding to cybercrime. Furthermore, over the past several years, many new anti-cybercrime statutes have been passed empowering federal, state, and local authorities to investigate and prosecute these crimes. But, law enforcement needs your help to stop the nefarious behavior of cyber criminals and bring them to justice.

Who to contact:

- **Local law enforcement.** Even if you have been the target of a multijurisdictional cybercrime, your local law enforcement agency (either police department or sheriff's office) has an obligation to assist you, take a formal report, and make referrals to other agencies, when appropriate. Report your situation as soon as you find out about it. Some local agencies have detectives or departments that focus specifically on cybercrime.

- **IC3.** The Internet Crime Complaint Center (IC3) will thoroughly review and evaluate your complaint and refer it to the appropriate federal, state, local, or international law enforcement or regulatory agency that has jurisdiction over the matter. IC3 is a partnership between the Federal Bureau of Investigation and the National White Collar Crime Center (funded, in part, by the Department of Justice's Bureau of Justice Assistance). Complaints may be filed online at http://www.ic3.gov/default.aspx.

- **Federal Trade Commission**. The FTC does not resolve individual consumer complaints, but does operate the Consumer Sentinel, a secure online database that is used by civil and criminal law enforcement authorities worldwide to detect patterns of wrong-doing, leading to investigations and prosecutions. File your complaint at https://www.ftccomplaintassistant.gov/FTC_Wizard.aspx?Lang=en. Victims of identity crime may receive additional help through the FTC hotline at 1-877-IDTHEFT (1-877-438-4388); the FTC website at www.ftc.gov/IDTheft provides resources for victims, businesses, and law enforcement.

Collect and Keep Evidence

Even though you may not be asked to provide evidence when you first report the cybercrime, it is very important to keep any evidence you may have related to your complaint. Keep items in a safe location in the event you are requested to provide them for investigative or prosecutive evidence. Evidence may include, but is not limited to, the following:

- Canceled checks
- Certified or other mail receipts
- Chatroom or newsgroup text
- Credit card receipts
- Envelopes (if you received items via FedEx, UPS, or U.S. Mail)
- Facsimiles

- Log files, if available, with date, time and time zone
- Messages from Facebook, Twitter or other social networking sites
- Money order receipts
- Pamphlets or brochures
- Phone bills
- Printed or preferably electronic copies of emails (if printed, include full email header information)
- Printed or preferably electronic copies of web pages
- Wire receipts

Additional Tips for Specific Types of Cybercrime

Once you discover that you have become a victim of cybercrime, your response will depend, to some degree, on the type and particular circumstances of the crime. Here are useful tips to follow for some specific types of cybercrimes:

In cases of identity theft:

- Make sure you change your passwords for all online accounts. When changing your password, make it long, strong and unique, with a mix of upper and lowercase letters, numbers and symbols. You also may need to contact your bank and other financial institutions to freeze your accounts so that the offender is not able to access your financial resources.
- Close any unauthorized or compromised credit or charge accounts. Cancel each credit and charge

card. Get new cards with new account numbers. Inform the companies that someone may be using your identity, and find out if there have been any unauthorized transactions. Close accounts so that future charges are denied. You may also want to write a letter to the company so there is a record of the problem.

- Think about what other personal information may be at risk. You may need to contact other agencies depending on the type of theft. For example, if a thief has access to your Social Security number, you should contact the Social Security Administration. You should also contact your state Department of Motor Vehicles if your driver's license or car registration is stolen.
- File a report with your local law enforcement agency. Even if your local police department or sheriff's office doesn't have jurisdiction over the crime (a common occurrence for online crime which may originate in another jurisdiction or even another country), you will need to provide a copy of the law enforcement report to your banks, creditors, other businesses, credit bureaus, and debt collectors.
- If your personal information has been stolen through a corporate data breach (when a cyber thief hacks into a large database of accounts to steal information, such as Social Security numbers, home addresses, and personal email addresses), you will likely be contacted by the business or agency whose data was compromised with additional instructions, as appropriate. You

may also contact the organization's IT security officer for more information.

- If stolen money or identity is involved, contact one of the three credit bureaus to report the crime (Equifax at 1-800-525-6285, Experian at 1-888-397-3742, or TransUnion at 1-800-680-7289). Request that the credit bureau place a fraud alert on your credit report to prevent any further fraudulent activity (such as opening an account with your identification) from occurring. As soon as one of the bureaus issues a fraud alert, the other two bureaus are automatically notified.

For additional resources, visit the Identity Theft Resource Center at www.idtheftcenter.org or the Federal Trade Commission at http://www.ftc.gov/bcp/edu/microsites/idtheft/tools.html.

In cases of Social Security fraud:

- If you believe someone is using your social security number for employment purposes or to fraudulently receive Social Security benefits, contact the Social Security Administration's fraud hotline at 1-800-269-0271. Request a copy of your social security statement to verify its accuracy.

For additional resources, visit the Social Security Administration at http://oig.ssa.gov/report-fraud-waste-or-abuse.

In cases of online stalking:

- In cases where the offender is known, send the stalker a clear written warning saying the contact is unwanted and asking that the perpetrator cease sending communications of any kind. Do this only once and do not communicate with the stalker again (Ongoing contact usually only encourages the stalker to continue the behavior).
    - Save copies of all communication from the stalker (e.g., emails, threatening messages, messages via social media) and document each contact, including dates, times and additional circumstances, when appropriate.
    - File a complaint with the stalker's Internet Service Provider (ISP) and yours. Many ISPs offer tools that filter or block communications from specific individuals.
    - Own your online presence. Set security and privacy settings on social networks and other services to your comfort level of sharing.
    - Consider changing your email address and ISP; use encryption software or privacy protection programs on your computer and mobile devices. (You should consult with law enforcement before changing your email account. It can be beneficial to the investigation to continue using the email account so law enforcement can also monitor communication.)
    - File a report with local law enforcement or contact your local prosecutor's office to see what charges, if any, can be pursued.

Stalking is illegal in all 50 states and the District of Columbia.

For additional resources, visit the Stalking Resource Center at www.ncvc.org/src.

In cases of cyberbullying:

- Tell a trusted adult about what's going on.
- Save any of the related emails, texts, or messages as evidence.
- Keep a record of incidents.
- Report the incident to the website's administrator; many websites including Facebook and YouTube encourage users to report incidents of cyberbullying.
- Block the person on social networks and in email.
- Avoid escalating the situation: Responding with hostility is likely to provoke a bully. Depending on the circumstances, consider ignoring the issue. Often, bullies thrive on the reaction of their victims. If you or your child receives unwanted email messages, consider changing your email address. The problem may stop. If you continue to get messages at the new account, you may have a strong case for legal action.
- If the communications become more frequent, the threats more severe, the methods more dangerous and if third-parties (such as hate groups and sexually deviant groups) become involved—the more likely law enforcement needs to be contacted and a legal process initiated.

For more information, visit www.stopcyberbullying.org and www.ncpc.org/cyberbullying

How Did This Happen To Me? A Word about Malware

Many cybercrimes start with malware—short for "malicious software." Malware includes viruses and spyware that get installed on your computer, phone, or mobile device without your consent—you may have downloaded the malware without even realizing it! These programs can cause your device to crash and can be used to monitor and control your online activity. Criminals use malware to steal personal information and commit fraud. If you think your computer has malware, you can file a complaint with the Federal Trade Commission at www.ftc.gov/complaint.

Avoid malware with the following tips from the STOP. THINK. CONNECT. campaign:

- Keep a clean machine by making sure your security software, operating system and web browser are up to date.
- When in doubt throw it out. Don't click on any links or open attachments unless you trust the source.
- Make your passwords long and strong and unique. Combine capital and lowercase letters with numbers and symbols to create a more secure password. Use a different password for each account.

69

- Set your browser security high enough to detect unauthorized downloads.
- Use a pop-up blocker (the links in pop-up ads are notorious sources of malware).
- Back up your data regularly (just in case your computer crashes).
- Protect all devices that connect to the Internet. Along with computers, smart phones, gaming systems, and other web-enabled devices also need protection from malware.
- Make sure all members of your family follow these safety tips (one infected computer on a home network can infect other computers).

Other Places to Find Resources or File a Complaint:

- Anti-Phishing Working Group (reportphishing@antiphishing.org)
- Better Business Bureau (investigates disagreements between businesses and customers; https://www.bbb.org/consumer-complaints/file-a-complaint/get-started)
- CyberTipLine, operated by the National Center for Missing & Exploited Children (investigates cases of online sexual exploitation of children; 1-800-843-5678 or www.cybertipline.com)
- Electronic Crimes Task Forces and Working Groups (http://www.secretservice.gov/ectf.shtml)
- The Secret Service (investigates fraudulent use of currency; http://www.secretservice.gov/field_offices.shtml)
- StopFraud.Gov Victims of Fraud Resources (http://www.stopfraud.gov/victims.html)

- U.S. Computer Emergency Readiness Team (www.us-cert.gov)
- U.S. Department of Justice (www.justice.gov/criminal/cybercrime)
- U.S. Postal Inspection Service (investigates fraudulent on-line auctions and other cases involving the mail; https://postalinspectors.uspis.gov/contactus/fileco mplaint.aspx)
- Your State Attorney General (the National Association of Attorneys General keeps a current contact list at http://www.naag.org/current-attorneys-general.php)

The National Cyber Security Alliance would like to thank the National Sheriffs' Association and International Association of Chiefs of Police for their assistance in creating this resource.

Chapter 6 – How to Become the Hunter & Not the Prey

ForensicsNation offers a program designed to turn everyday internet users into amateur Internet sleuths. The program is inexpensive and pretty comprehensive. Go here and check it out:

ForensicsNation Bushwhacker Program
http://www.amazon.com/dp/B007I9AHVS

Here is an excerpt from the book:
ForensicsNation Bushwhacker Program

©2014 Dr. Leland Benton

> **"Any sufficiently advanced technology is indistinguishable from magic."**
>
> *- Arthur C. Clarke*

Introduction

Welcome to ForensicsNation. I'm Dr. Leland Benton and I am the Chief Forensics Investigator for ForensicsNation. My company – Neternatives.com – is actually made up of 32-divisons with ForensicsNation being the largest. As the Managing Director of Neternatives, I wear many hats but the one that keeps me the most active is forensics. I am the public voice or mouthpiece for the company. Because of the nature of our business, our forensic investigators remain behind a screen of anonymity. We work mostly out of a series of control rooms. Our computer systems are second to none and we track cyber-crime worldwide.

I create the software programs that catch bad guys. I also create the methods and modalities ForensicsNation uses to identify the bad guys and compile evidence against them.

Forensics, by definition, is the identification of the perpetrators of crime and the compilation of evidence against them. We aren't some cyber-NCIS or Dog the Bounty Hunter nor do we have any police authority to arrest the criminals that we find. Our job is to find them, compile the evidence against them and then turn it over to law enforcement or whomever has hired us such as large corporations, individuals, bounty hunters, bail bondsmen, etc.

The ForensicsNation Bushwhacker Program is like nothing you have ever seen before. You may be selling a Clickbank diet program online and making a $50 commission and that's okay. I catch bad guys and collect very large rewards and once you learn my trade you will see just how profitable it is and can be for you. Where to you find perpetrators with rewards on their heads?

Here's one site and there are hundreds of sites like this that we identify for you in our program:

http://www.mostwantedhoes.com/rewards/

The ForensicsNation Bushwhacker Program is made up of two parts.

The ForensicsNation Bushwhacker Program teaches you how to protect yourself and your loved ones from cyber attacks, identity theft, hacking, and more. You are also taught to basically become an amateur Internet sleuth. We will supply you with the tools; most of them are free and some you have to pay for and we also provide you with a checklist where you can offer your services to small local businesses and individual to protect them from cyber attacks too.

So, just how vulnerable are YOU? I am going to demonstrate your cyber-vulnerability but I am warning you in advance that this is happening every day!

Your websites – most of you reading this own Wordpress blogs. It takes less than 30-seconds to break into a blog's WP Admin area using a free software program available on torrent sites. I will show you a four-digit code to add to your blog's username that will prevent any bad guy breaking into your admin area and wreaking havoc before you even know you have been penetrated. BTW – I caught one clever bad guy who broke into an admin area of a very big online marketer and changed the PayPal account username directing all of the sales to his PayPal account. By the time this was discovered he had made off with over $250,000 in sales. Yes, we tracked him down and he was prosecuted and most of the money was recovered but not all of it.

Your personal information – with our company's proprietary software, it takes me all of 10-minutes to compile a dossier on you complete with all of your bank accounts, investment accounts, driver's license, social security number, personal information such as family members, their names and personal info, property records, cars you own, and much more. In fact, the amount of information I can compile on you is almost endless and it is your fault because you placed this information or allowed it to be placed on the Internet without even realizing how vulnerable it makes you. I will show you how to protect your identity and literally drop off the grid. In conjunction with one of our sister divisions – **PrivacyNations** – I will also show you how to make your information inaccessible.

Your location – if you carry a cell phone, a driver's license or use your car, I know where you are and where you have been 24/7. Every cell phone has a GPS tracking chip in it (not just the smart phones; the analog phones too), every driver's license now has a RFID chip in it that works off the cell phone antennas, and the new cars have GPS locators in them like the GM OnStar. You can remove the battery from your cell phone to disable the GPS function but there is nothing you can do about your driver's license.

If you are an online marketer dealing in mobile commerce, you have probably heard of a GPS Fence. You can "tag" a business with a GPS tag and when any of the business owner's customers comes within 300-yards of the business, a text message is triggered to the customer's cell phone. In forensics, we have what is called GPS Laser tagging where I can place a tag on any physical object and track it by satellite through one of our divisions – **TheoSat** – so there is nowhere to hide, people! How do you think the feds catch bad guys so quickly? Now the really tech savvy bad guys know all of what I have just taught you and more and they know how to protect themselves but everybody slips up and when they do I own them!

   Your physical well-being - GPS is a good thing when used properly. One of our divisions – **PinpointProtect** - offers GPS protection services to high profile people, people who travel extensively, women, children, and anyone vulnerable to physical attack or abduction. Each person is given a tracker to carry and the tracker has an SOS button so when they get into trouble they can just push the SOS button. Our control room tracks them and then provides whatever services are required to assist the person. Each person is also given an Internet Interface where they can dial in and see where they are 24/7. If they get lost, they can easily find out there location and how to get to where they are supposed to be. They can give their login coordinates to anyone they choose – wife, parents, etc – and these people can login and find out where they are 24/7. Yes, GPS does have its useful purposes. One customer of ours is a game hunter and he got lost in Alaska. He hit the SOS button and he was rescued within 2-hours.

   And it is not just individuals that are vulnerable. You all have heard of the hacking group "Anonymous" that hacked the financial institutions that refused to do business with Wikileaks. This same group threatened the Mexican Drug Cartels when the cartels captured one of their members. DUMB...real dumb! I do TV, radio and magazine interviews weekly. I was asked to comment on Anonymous going after the Mexican Drug Cartels. Here is the article. Slide down the page; my comment was quite short:

http://www.dailydot.com/news/anonymous-mexico-opcorrupcion/

There is a good deal of stuff to get to in The ForensicsNation Bushwhacker Program so be prepared to study. This guidebook will cover computer investigation, Internet investigation, and Internet forensics. I have left all of the resources from the first program intact because you will need them. I have added some resources that were not available to the first program users. At the very end of this guidebook, I have included a Bonus Section. I have taken information from our sister division – **PrivacyNations.com** – and included it since their programs and products are highly synergistic with ForensicsNation and you will undoubtedly be incorporating its product lines into your services...enjoy!

We are going to be talking in the context of running an Internet investigation and forensics business. I am going to outline for you what is needed and as we go along this will give you the ability to compile a checklist.

There are many aspects to this business. You may incorporate all of them or pick and choose the ones that best suit your talents and passions. I don't expect you to turn it into a behemoth that ForensicsNation has become but it certainly possible and the market demand for what we do is growing faster than we can provide services. But note, a good many aspects of this business will not become available to you without the proper training so pay close attention to the Continuing Education and Certification section below.

We are going to discuss business structure, licensing, insurance, continuing education, certification, and marketing throughout this course and a bunch of other stuff too. Please do not cut any corners; everything I discuss is essential in protecting you and your business as well as maximizing the profit potential.

Business Structure

The way you structure your forensics business is important. Do not operate as a sole proprietor. The best way is a limited liability corporation (LLC) and the best place to incorporate is Nevada.

Please be sure to consult an attorney. You will need an attorney to assist you in issuing subpoenas, and you will also need an attorney specializing in Federal law too. I would pay close attention to selecting an attorney and get their fee schedule up front. They will be a big part of your business so the attorney's availability is important. Ask questions! Can his paralegal prepare and issue subpoenas? Once you begin operations, you will identify other legal needs as well.

In the Bonus Section, there is more information on Nevada LLCs.

Insurance

A good insurance agent will advise you on the appropriate coverages. Be sure to make it known to your insurance agent that you ARE NOT a field investigator and the majority of your work will be from your home/office on your computer.

You will need a very good general liability policy with $1-million in coverage and if you can qualify for it, you will also need a $5-million Umbrella Policy.

Don't forget to insurance all of your equipment and computer plus all of your software too.

Products & Services

Here is a <u>partial</u> list of products and services you can provide:

Computer/Internet Forensics

Data Recovery
Internet Fraud Investigations
Other Computer Related Crimes
Theft of Trade Secrets or Intellectual Property
Internet Related Fraud
Theft of Trade Secrets
Criminal Activities
Hacking
Theft
Fraud
Forensic Computer Examinations
Computer Data Forensic Analysis
Lost Data Recovery
Hidden Data Recovery
"Exact" Copies of Hard Disks and Computer Media
Unlocking Passwords and Lost Password Recovery

Digital Discovery for Law Firms and Litigation
Data Authentication
Data Format Conversion
"Suspect Employee" Internal Corporate Inquiries
"Trojan Horse" Hijacked Computer Analysis
Deleted E-mail and Instant Message Chat recovery
Kazaa/Morpheus/Grokster (etc.) file sharing analysis
ICQ / AOL Instant Message / Yahoo / MSN6 and similar
instant message chat recovery and analysis
Internet History and Web Surfing Activity Analysis
Data Recovery from Damaged Floppies and CD-Rs
Wipe ("sterilize") old hard drives to DOD Standards
Computer Registry Analysis

Internet Investigations

Email Tracing
Email search
Finding people
Background check
Address search
Public record search
Criminal record search
DMV record check
Court record search
Adoptee search
Birth mother search
Property record search
Death records search
Employee Internet Abuse
Pornography and Child Pornography Issues
Identity Theft Investigations
Suspected Spousal Infidelity

Network or System Intrusion Detection
Internet or Email Harassment Cases
Nigerian (419) Scams
Spousal Infidelity Issues
Corporate Due Diligence
Jury Member Screening
Asset Searches
Intellectual Property Issues
Missing Person Locates
Internet Expert Witness Services
Internet Defamation
Stalking
Incident Response
Litigation Support
Website tracing

Computer Investigation

Keystroke logging - (often called keylogging) is the action of tracking (or logging) the keys struck on a keyboard, typically in a covert manner so that the person using the keyboard is unaware that their actions are being monitored. There are numerous keylogging methods, ranging from hardware and software-based approaches to electromagnetic and acoustic analysis.

Counter forensics - (sometimes counter forensics) is a general term for a set of techniques used as countermeasures to forensic analysis.

Cryptanalysis - where it is obvious that intercepted data contains a message (though that message is encrypted)

Data remanence - is the residual representation of data that remains even after attempts have been made to remove or erase the data.

Disk encryption - uses disk encryption software or hardware to encrypt every bit of data that goes on a disk or disk volume. Disk encryption prevents unauthorized access to data storage. The term "full disk encryption" (or whole disk encryption) is often used to signify that everything on a disk is encrypted, including the programs that can encrypt bootable operating system partitions. But they must still leave the master boot record (MBR), and thus part of the disk, unencrypted. There are, however, hardware-based full disk encryption systems that can truly encrypt the entire boot disk, including the MBR.

Encryption - is the process of transforming information (referred to as plaintext) using an algorithm (called a cipher) to make it unreadable to anyone except those possessing special knowledge, usually referred to as a key.

Hidden file and hidden directory - a hidden directory or hidden file on a computer is a directory (folder) or file which a user cannot see by default. Hidden directories most often serve to hide important operating system-related files and user preferences. However, malicious programs can also use this functionality to hide their presence from unaware users.
Information technology audit - An information technology audit, or information systems audit, is an examination of the management controls within an Information technology (IT) infrastructure. The

evaluation of obtained evidence determines if the information systems are safeguarding assets, maintaining data integrity, and operating effectively to achieve the organization's goals or objectives. These reviews may be performed in conjunction with a financial statement audit, internal audit, or other form of attestation engagement.

Steganalysis - The goal of steganalysis is to identify suspected packages, determine whether or not they have a payload encoded into them, and, if possible, recover that payload.

Pricing

Pricing varies by location and competition. On the forensics side, there is virtually no competition. My people bill out at $250/hour - $350/hour for forensics. When we do a business analysis and protect their computers, we charge a flat fee of $25/computer.

Fees are normally based upon an hourly rate of $250 to $350 per hour, depending upon the operating system, the difficulty of the examination or recovery, and whether court testimony may be necessary. This rate should be determined and quoted before any limited or complete examination begins.

Four types of examinations: (1) a preliminary evaluation for $600 to determine whether further examination is advisable, (2) an intermediate, limited examination of 10 to 20 hours for finding specific items of interest to the client (the time may increase or decrease based on the operating system, hardware difficulties encountered, multiple hard drives encountered, the number of floppies or other media to be examined, password or encryption problems to be resolved, the type of data encountered, or other specific examination requirements made by the client), (3) a complete examination of up to 35 billable hours (which may increase or decrease for reasons similar to those mentioned above), and (4) a complete data audit/digital autopsy of the hard drive or other media. (A complete data audit or digital autopsy identifies and catalogs every existing type of data on a hard disk drive and presents a detailed and exhaustive report to the client or to the courts.)

Retainer: A retainer of 50% of the estimated examination cost is required before the limited or complete examination is started. A signed retention agreement is required before conducting an examination. The retention agreement specifies the scope and details of the examination to be performed.

Travel rates: Our out-of-town daily rate is 2 times the quoted hourly rate, plus reasonable per diem and expenses. The in-town travel rate is 1/2 the quoted hourly rate.

In the past, Computer Forensic Examinations could run tens of thousands of dollars because of the manpower necessary to thoroughly examine a hard-drive. With the advancement of technology in the Computer Forensics arena that is no longer the case. The software and hardware available now make the price of Computer Forensics affordable and well worth the investment. The prices can range from $250/hour to $350/hour and the process involves basically three steps: Acquisition, Investigation, and Reporting. Acquisitions usually cost less than $500.00. Investigation and Reporting, of course, depend on the nature of your case. In most instances, searching and reporting can be completed in less than 15 hours and the total analysis is usually less than $4500.00.

Licensing

I know of no particular licensing requirements but to be safe check with your state and local authorities. You are not a field investigator nor are you a bounty hunter. You will work with these people but you do not have any contact with perpetrators with the exception of going to court to testify. If you seriously apply yourself to this business and garner the necessary certifications as listed in the Education section, then you will qualify as an expert witness and the fees are enormous. I charge $500/hour to testify in court.

Continuing Education & Certification

There is no silver-bullet certification available for forensic investigators, but apart from the Certified Information Systems Security Professional (CISSP) there are a few other diverse, vendor-neutral certifications for those who wish to establish and enhance their skill sets.

Certified Information Forensics Investigator (CIFI) - Offered by the International Information Systems Forensics Association, CIFI is designed to demonstrate expertise in all aspects of the information investigative process.

http://www.infoforensics.org

Certified Forensic Computer Examiner (CFCE) and Certified Electronic Evidence Collection Specialist (CEECS) - Offered by the International Association of Computer Investigative Specialists. CFCE and CEECS are forensic certifications offered for law enforcement officers. http://www.cops.org/cfce.htm

GIAC Certified Forensic Analyst (GCFA) - Offered by the SANS Institute's Global Information Assurance Certification group, GCFA tests the knowledge and skills to handle forensic scenarios, incident investigations, and forensic investigation of networks.
http://www.giac.org/certifications/security/gcfa.php

Advanced Information Security & Assurance (AIS) - Offered by the Security University, AIS is an eight-module certification focusing on distinct skill sets within computer security. Although the certification is not just for forensics there is a strong forensic component.
http://www.securityuniversity.net

EnCE - The EnCase Certified Examiner Program offers certifications for those who have mastered their EnCase Guidance Software. Training courses and a copy of the software are required to gain the certification. This program is very reasonably priced at $200 for the exam (available through Prometric).
http://www.guidancesoftware.com/training/EnCE_certification.aspx

Computer Forensic External Certification (CCE) - Originally designed for law enforcement by the IACIS, this certification is now open to those with the experience and knowledge to complete the rigorous testing. The exam costs $750.
http://www.cops.org/External%20Certification.htm

Q/FE Qualified Forensics Expert - This less of a traditional certification than an in-depth training class with an exam and certificate at the end. The materials included will prepare you to find the cause of attack, compile evidence, and handle corporate repercussions. The cost of the course is US $2,995
http://www.securityuniversity.net/certification.htm

TruSecure ICSA Certified Security Associate - Although it is not directly a forensics certification, this overall security certification is highly respected and covers essential forensics procedures.
http://www.icsalabs.com/icsa/topic.php?tid=fdghgf54645
-ojojoj567

CCE - Certified Computer Examiner - You'll get a full dose of the technical side of data recovery and handling, but this certification stresses the importance of "following sound evidence handling and storage procedures and following sound examination procedures". The exam is $395 and many self-study materials are available.
http://www.certified-computer-examiner.com/

Computer Forensic Training Online - Get online training and CCE certification through Kennesaw State University. The course fee is $2700.

http://www.kennesaw.edu/coned/sci/for_online.htm

Here are sites to checkout:

http://www.giac.org/certification/certified-forensic-analyst-gcfa
http://www.acfei.com/
http://www.infosecinstitute.com/courses/computer_forensics_training.html

Marketing

This is the fun part....marketing. I may wear a good many hats and have a good load of responsibilities but marketing means fun to me because it is the action that makes everything happens.

First of all, since forensics is an unusual business and thanks to television, it carries an enormous amount of public awareness and respect. When someone asks you what you do and you tell them you are an Internet Forensics Investigator, you can be sure a conversation will follow.

What this means is that the marketing side is easy and you are not considered another salesman or solicitor. Your profession demands respect!

Here is a partial list of your main customers:

Law Firms
Accountants, Fraud Examiners and Auditors
Businesses and Corporations

Law Enforcement, Police Agencies and Prosecutors
Courts and the Judiciary (as a neutral third-party expert to the Court or a Special Master)
Private Investigators
Insurance Companies
Victims of Computer Crimes or Torts
Students or others suffering data loss

It would be advisable to prepare a nice brochure with all of your services and contact information. The customers listed above always have more work than investigators so be prepared to get a high influx of business. Only list the services you are interested in doing. Unless you take some training courses, some of what is listed is out of your realm of expertise…

*****

As you can see, it is quite a comprehensive program and one that you would be wise to consider.

That pretty much sums up what needs to be said about ForensicsNet™ /ForensicsLab™. I sincerely hope you take advantage of the resources I have provided by ForensicsNation. They are a company committed to your online security.

And be sure to join the notification list that will announce the public launch of ForensicsNet™ /ForensicsLab™.

My best to you all and now read on because I have a special gift for all of my readers.

I Have a Special Gift for My Readers

I appreciate my readers for without them I am just another author attempting to make a difference. If my book has made a favorable impression please leave me an honest review. Thank you in advance for you participation.

My readers and I have in common a passion for the written word as well as the desire to learn and grow from books.

My special offer to you is a massive ebook library that I have compiled over the years. It contains hundreds of fiction and non-fiction ebooks in Adobe Acrobat PDF format as well as the Greek classics and old literary classics too.

In fact, this library is so massive to completely download the entire library will require over 5 GBs open on your desktop.

Use the link below and scan all of the ebooks in the library. You can select the ebooks you want individually or download the entire library.

The link below does not expire after a given time period so you are free to return for more books rather than clog your desktop. And feel free to give the link to your friends who enjoy reading too.

I thank you for reading my book and hope if you are pleased that you will leave me an honest review so that I can improve my work and or write books that appeal to your interests.

Okay, here is the link…

http://tinyurl.com/special-readers-promo

PS: If you wish to reach me personally for any reason you may simply write to mailto:support@epubwealth.com.

I answer all of my emails so rest assured I will respond.

Meet the Author

Dr. Treat Preston is a behavioral scientist specializing in all types of relationships and associated problems, psychological triggers as applied to commercial advertising and marketing, and energy psychology. He is a best-selling author with numerous books dealing on publishing, behavioral science, marketing and more. He is also one of the lead research scientists with AppliedMindSciences.com, the mind research unit of ForensicsNation.com.

He and his wife Cynthia reside in Auburn, California.

Visit some of his websites
http://www.AddMeInNow.com
http://www.AppliedMindSciences.com
http://www.BookbuilderPLUS.com
http://www.BookJumping.com
http://www.EmailNations.com
http://www.EmbarrassingProblemsFix.com
http://www.ePubWealth.com
http://www.ForensicsNation.com
http://www.ForensicsNationStore.com
http://www.FreebiesNation.com
http://www.HealthFitnessWellnessNation.com
http://www.Neternatives.com
http://www.PrivacyNations.com
http://www.RetireWithoutMoney.org
http://www.SurvivalNations.com
http://www.TheBentonKitchen.com
http://www.Theolegions.org

http://www.VideoBookbuilder.com

Some Other Books You May Enjoy From ePubWealth.com, LLC Library Catalog

EPW Library Catalog Online
http://www.epubwealth.com/wp-content/uploads/2013/07/Leland-benton-private-turbo.pdf

EPW Library Catalog Download
http://www.filefactory.com/f/562ef3ea1a054f0a

www.ingramcontent.com/pod-product-compliance
Lightning Source LLC
LaVergne TN
LVHW052308060326
832902LV00021B/3769